The brand-name products mentioned in this publication are trademarks or service marks of their respective companies. The mention of any product in this publication does not constitute an endorsement by the respective proprietors of Publications International, Ltd., nor does it constitute an endorsement by any of these companies that their products should be used in the manner recommended by this publication.

New Seasons is a trademark of Publications International, Ltd.

© 2006 New Seasons
All rights reserved.
This publication may not be reproduced in whole or in part by any means whatsoever without written permission from:

Louis Weber, CEO
Publications International, Ltd.
7373 North Cicero Avenue
Lincolnwood, Illinois 60712

www.pilbooks.com

Permission is never granted for commercial purposes.

Manufactured in China.

8 7 6 5 4 3 2 1

ISBN: 1-4127-5310-4

HAVE A NICE DAY!

Laughter cures all

of life's bumps and bruises.

Hold hands with **your future.**

Nothing makes it **"ALL BETTER"** like a HUG FROM GRANDMA.

Every Wednesday afternoon, Spike **BABYSAT** the kids until Mrs. McInerny got back from the beauty shop.

It's easier to **SUCCEED** when EVERYONE'S PULLING for you.

"*Whatever* it is,

NEITHER of us did it."

Make a DATE with your INNER CHILD.

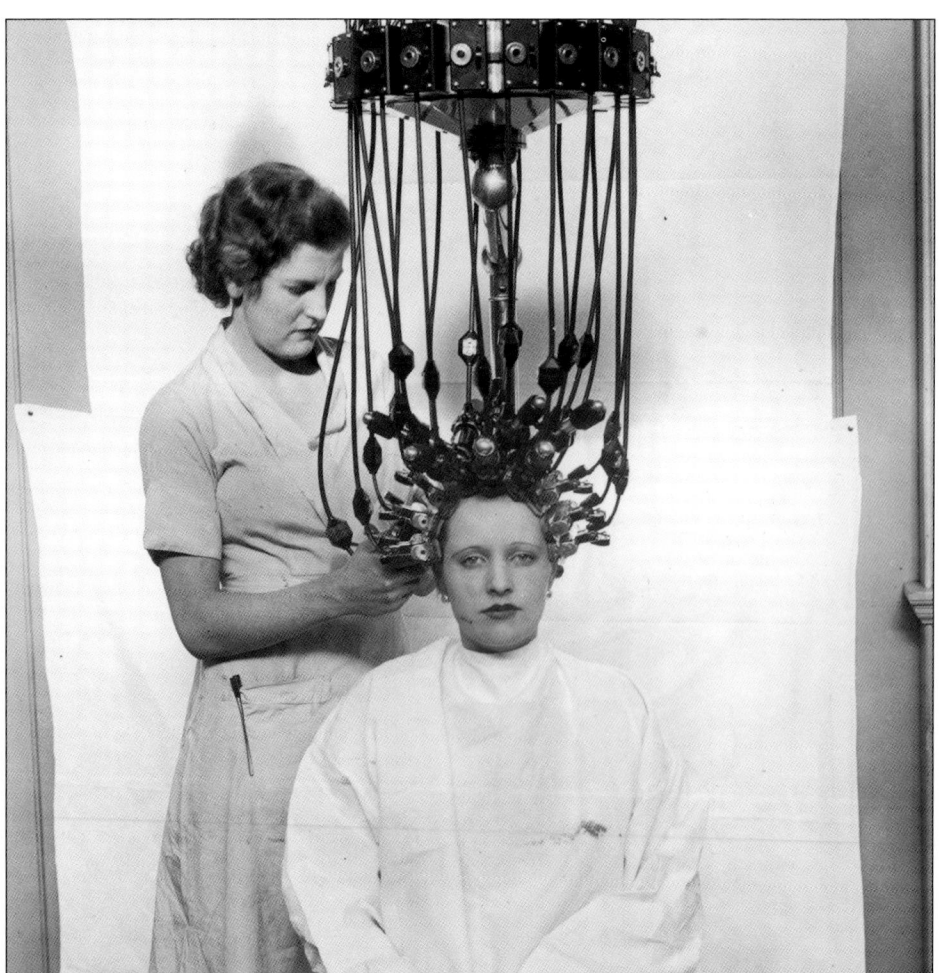

With the new Electro-curler, you can **KISS** both your BAD HAIR DAYS *and* your SHORT-TERM MEMORY **GOOD-BYE!**

Sometimes life **HANGS** you out **TO DRY.**

Always **SEPARATE** yourself from the FLOCK.

When your life becomes a **ROLLER COASTER**, get your best friend and sit in the **FRONT SEAT.**

Don't let OBSTACLES squash your ENTHUSIASM.

Ice cream makes a smile sweeter.

Surprise someone you love with a

SHOWER OF AFFECTION.

Never settle for the garden-variety.

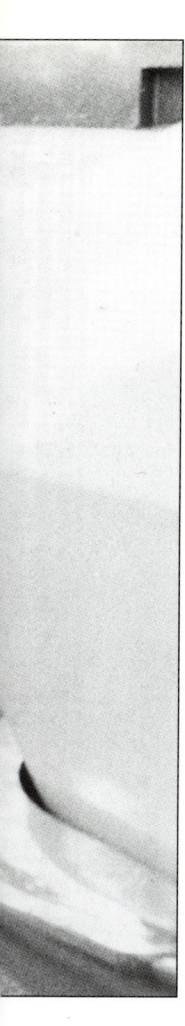

Y̲ou're **NEVER TOO YOUNG**

to learn how to **PARALLEL PARK.**

It's a BIG WORLD out there.

Bring **CHAPERONES**.

Say it with a CARD.

Say it with FLOWERS.

BUT SAY IT.

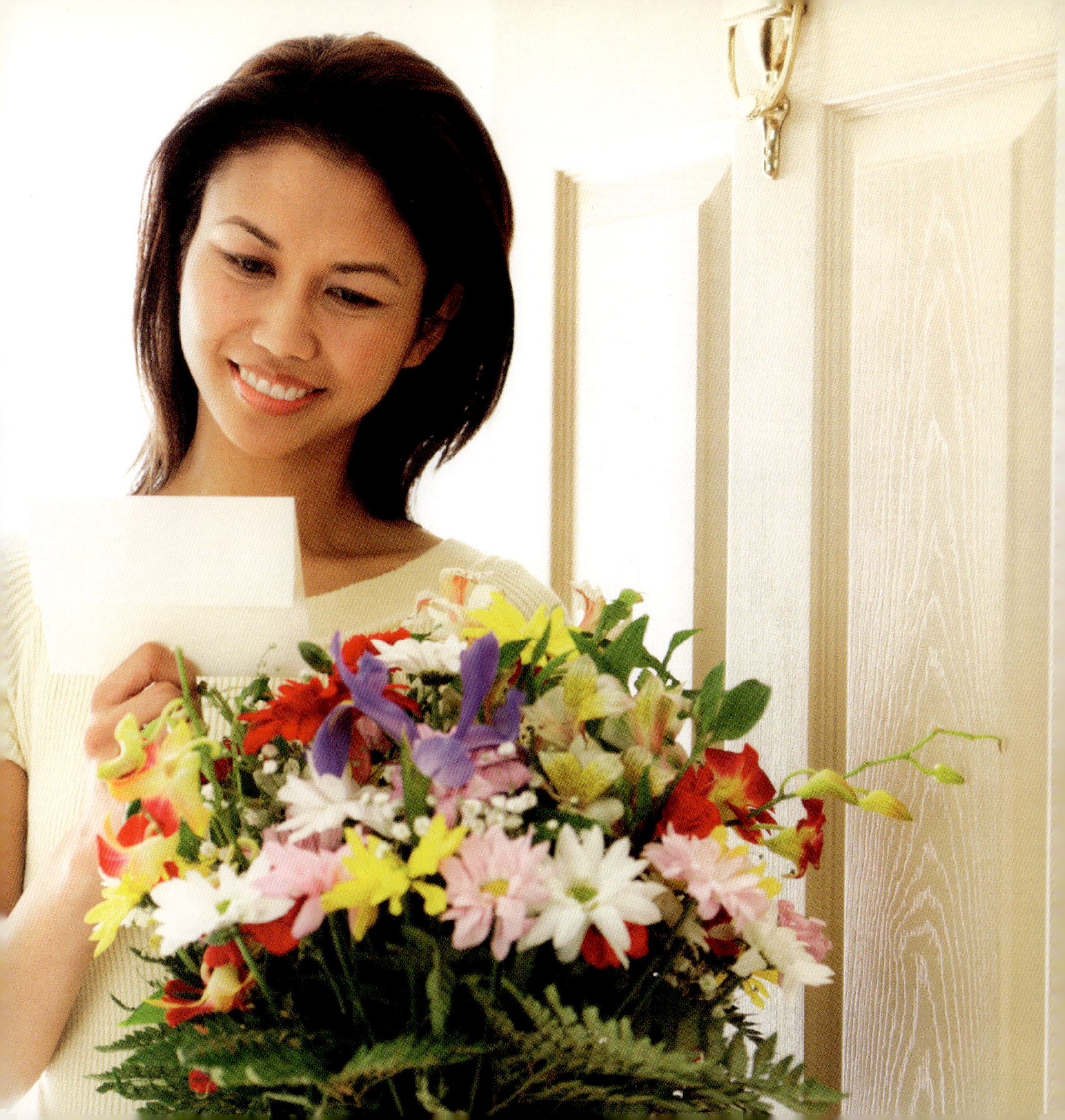

The **FIRST DAY** of anything can be a LITTLE STRESSFUL.

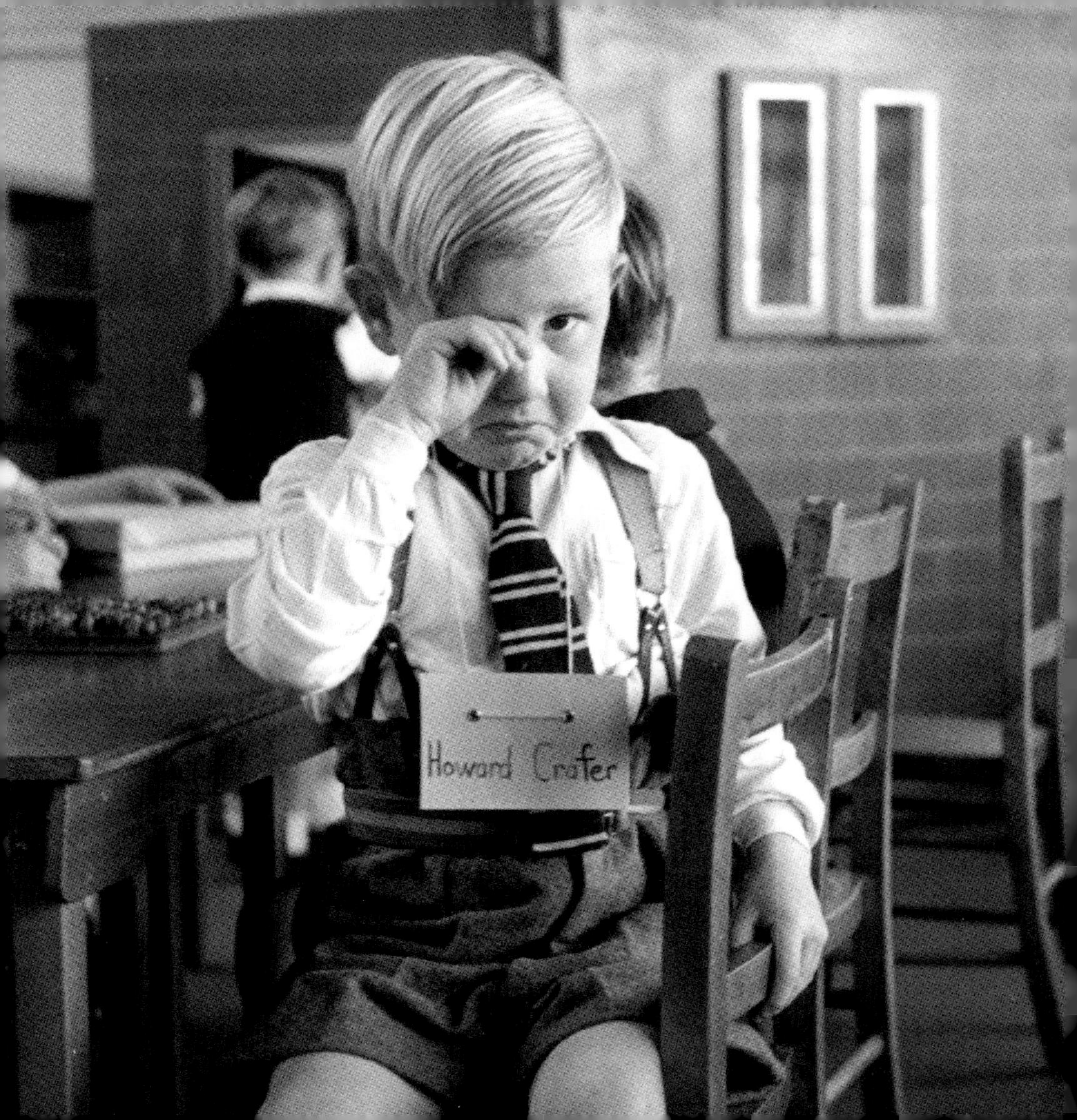
Howard Crafer

236, 35, 51 et 52
261, 76, 53
vente aux
Grossistes
87
Pati Pat
Prêt à Porter
STYLE JEUNE

Sometimes you're

SANDWICHED BETWEEN

your dreams and reality.

Sometimes you're

SANDWICHED BETWEEN

sandwiches.

And sometimes you're

THE SANDWICH.

"Oh, say can you see, by the dawn's early light...." GRANDMA LISTENED through THREE VERSES and never once thought about the PHONE BILL.

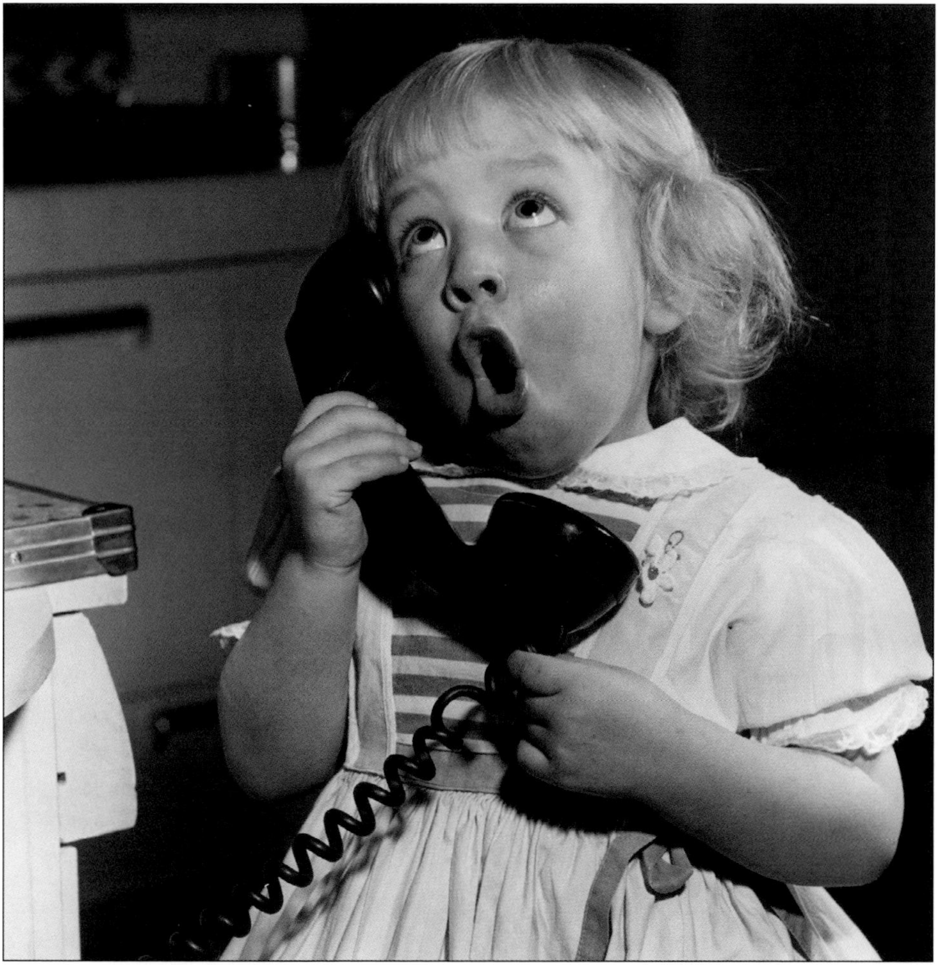

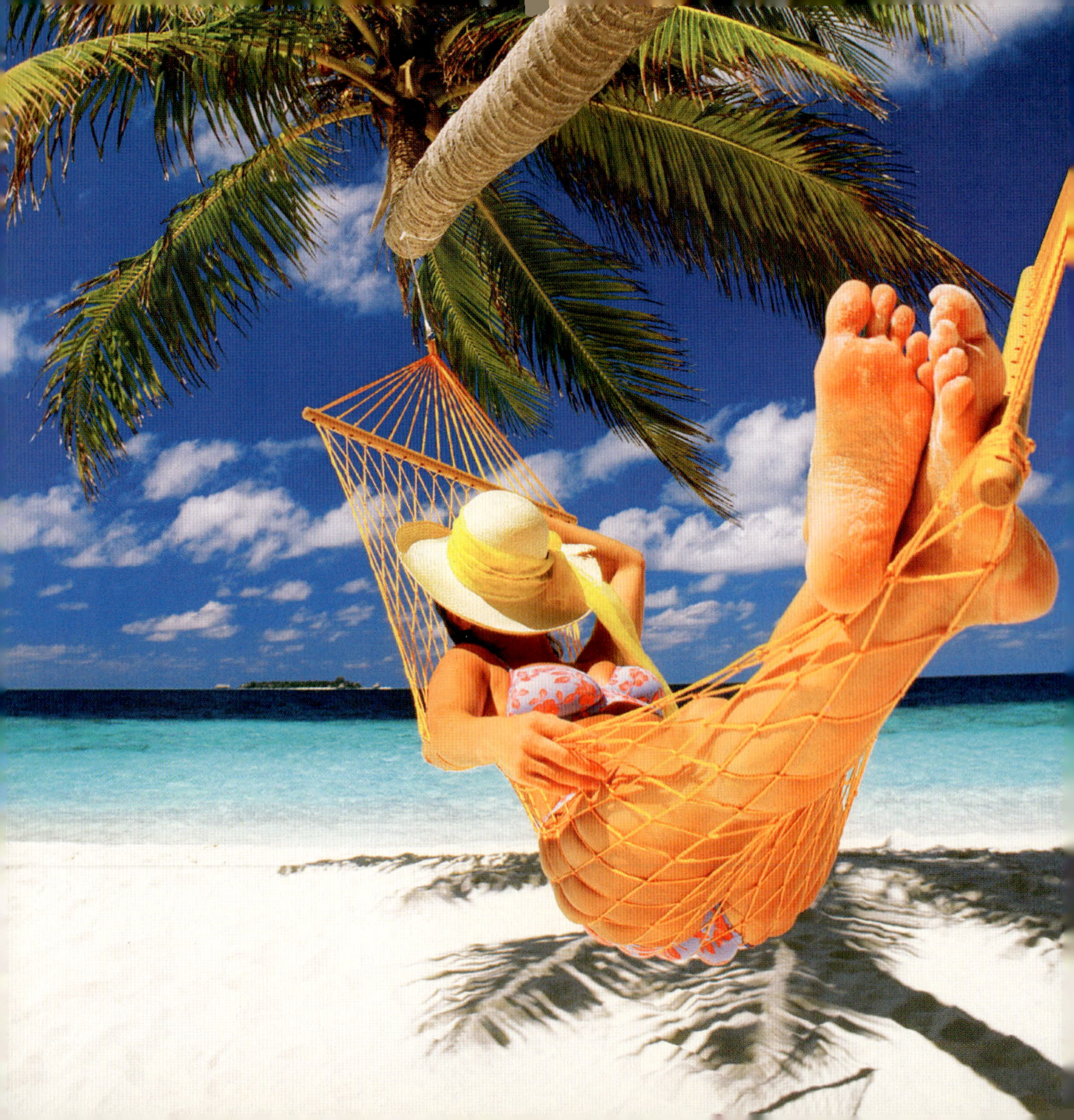

Sun. Surf. Sand.

Sensational.

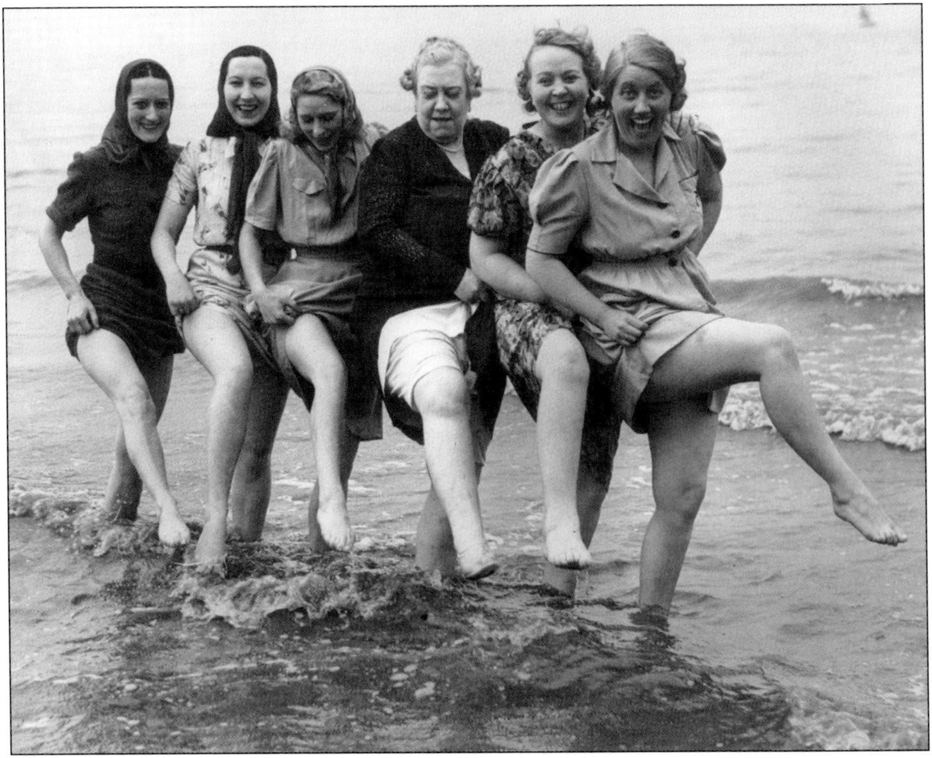

Doing the Cancun CANCAN!

"One for ME,

one for YOU."

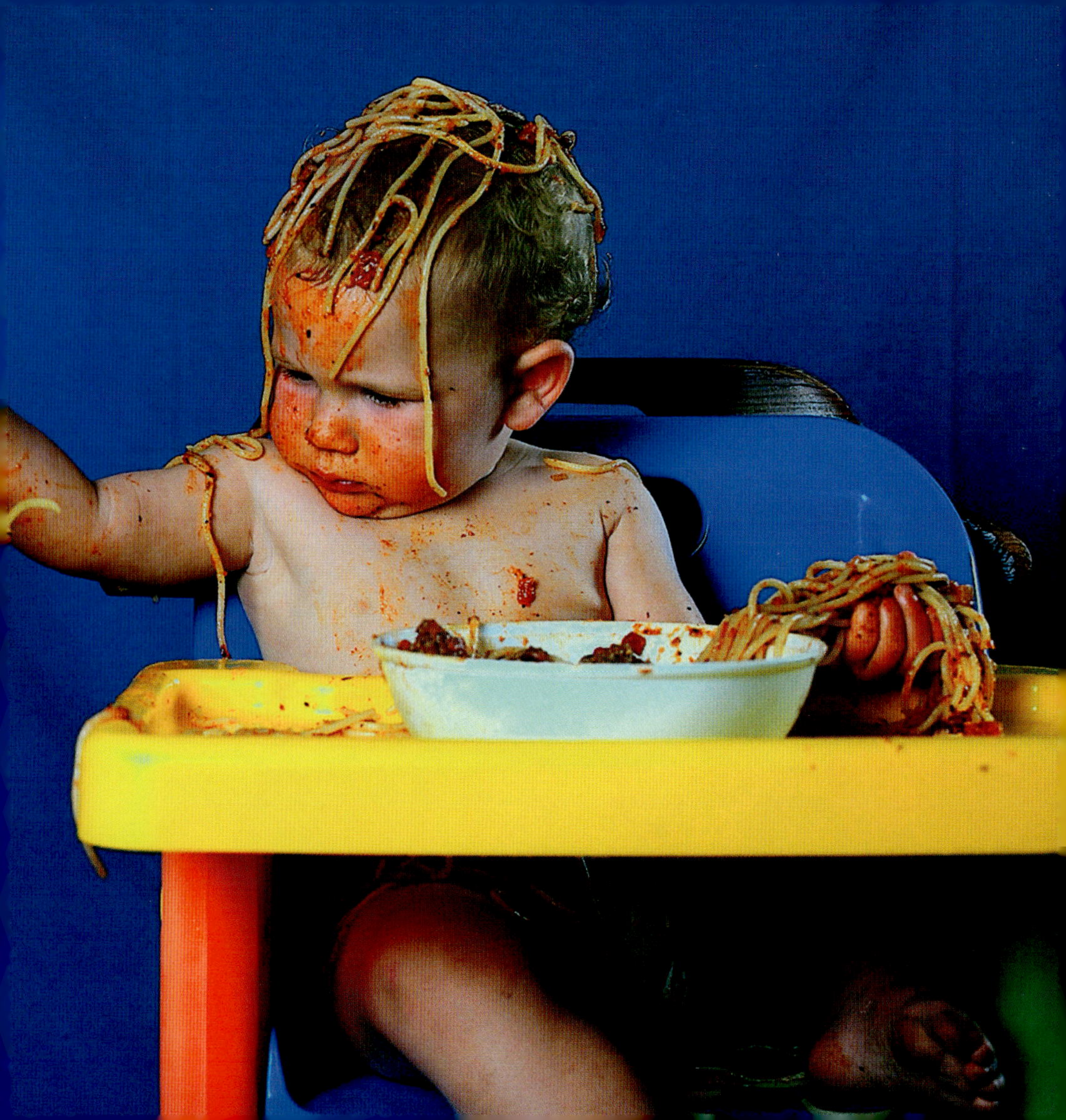

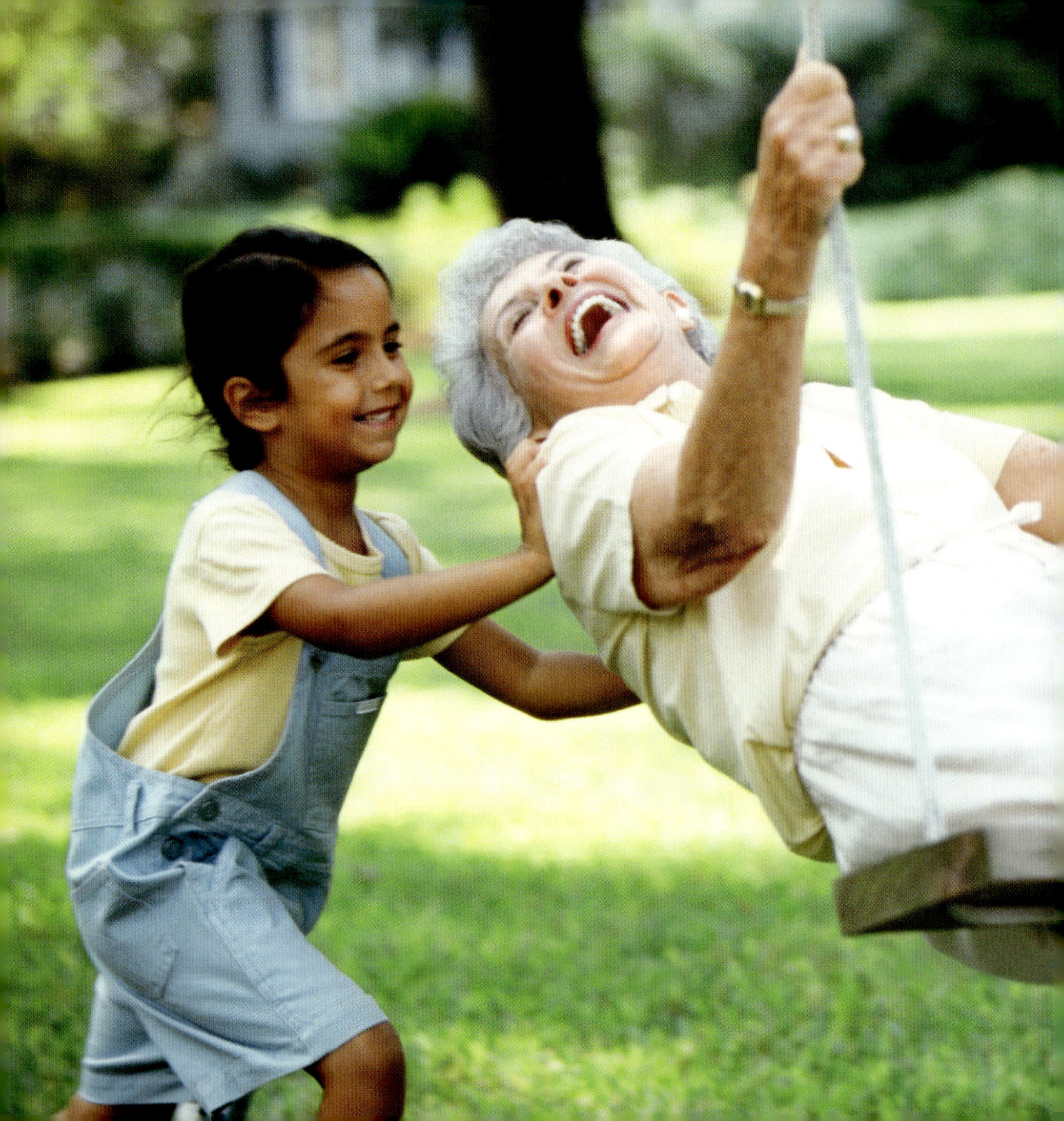

Turnabout

is **fair play!**

Your TALENT may be unusual, but *always* MAKE THE MOST of it.

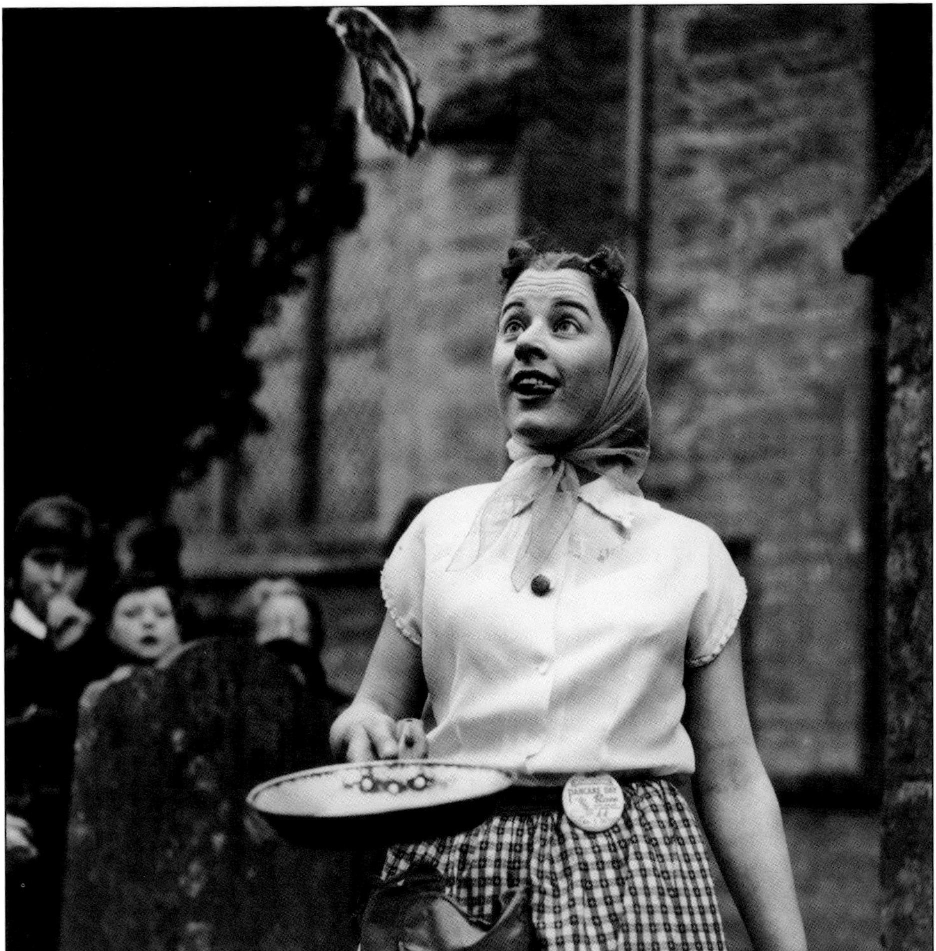
PANCAKE DAY
Race

You know it's a **ROUGH DAY** when even your TOYS TURN against you.

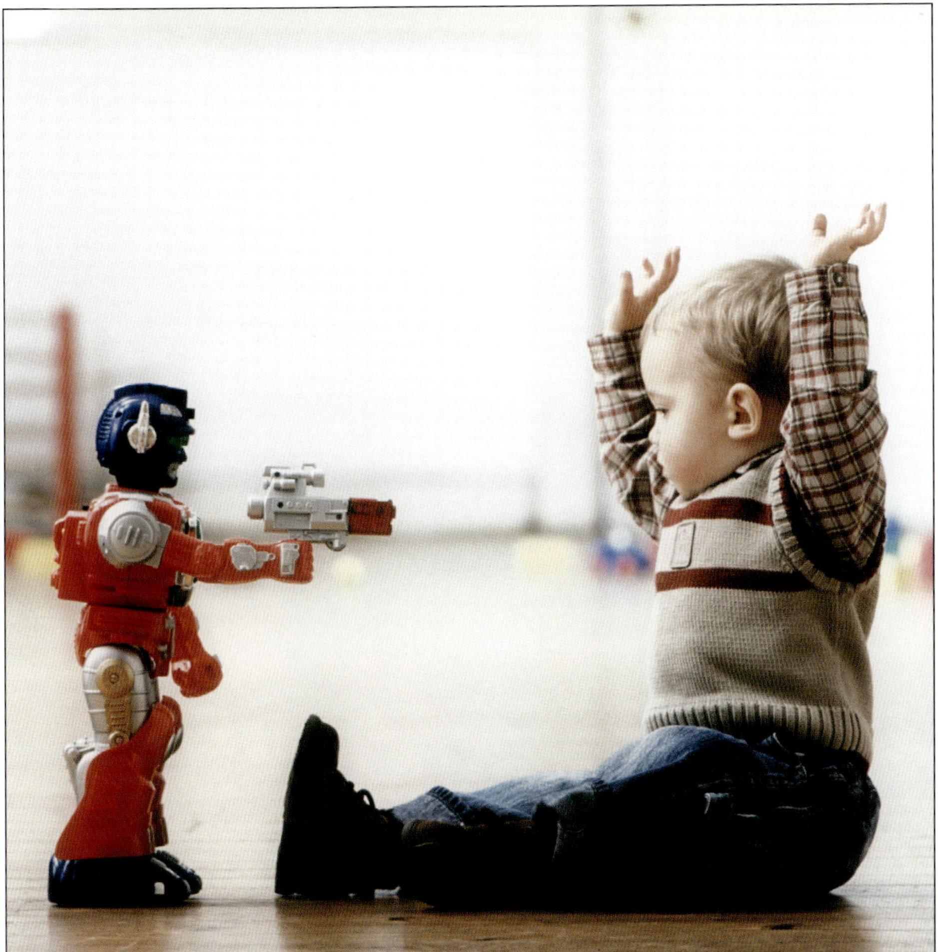

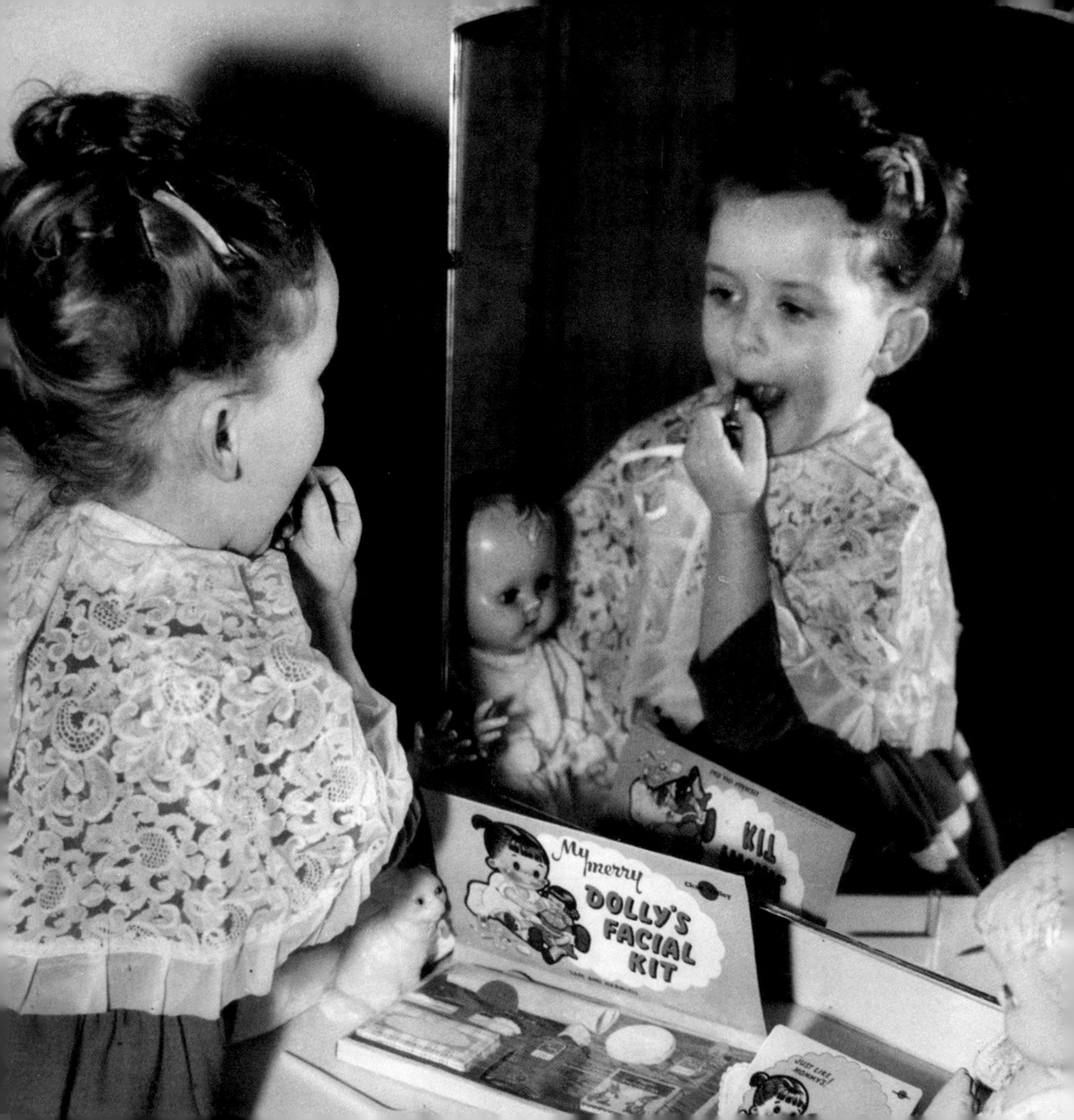
My merry
DOLLY'S
FACIAL
KIT
JUST LIKE MOMMY'S!

How do you get to be an **Avon lady?**

PRACTICE, **PRACTICE,** PRACTICE.

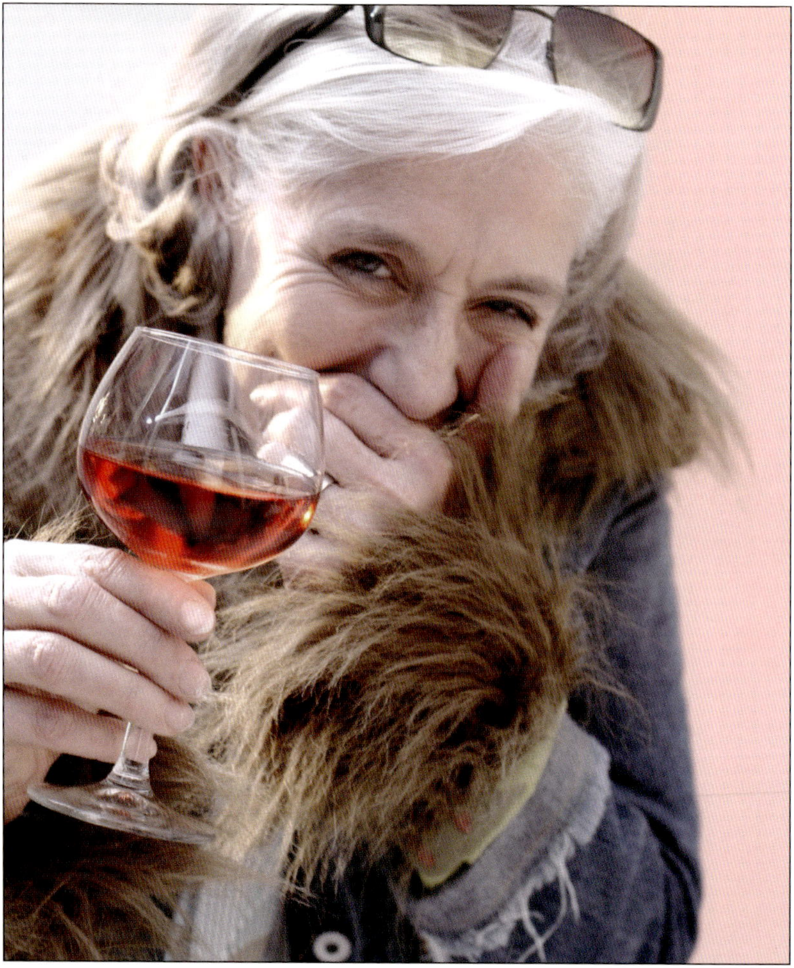

"My husband **THINKS** I'm at **BRIDGE CLUB.**"

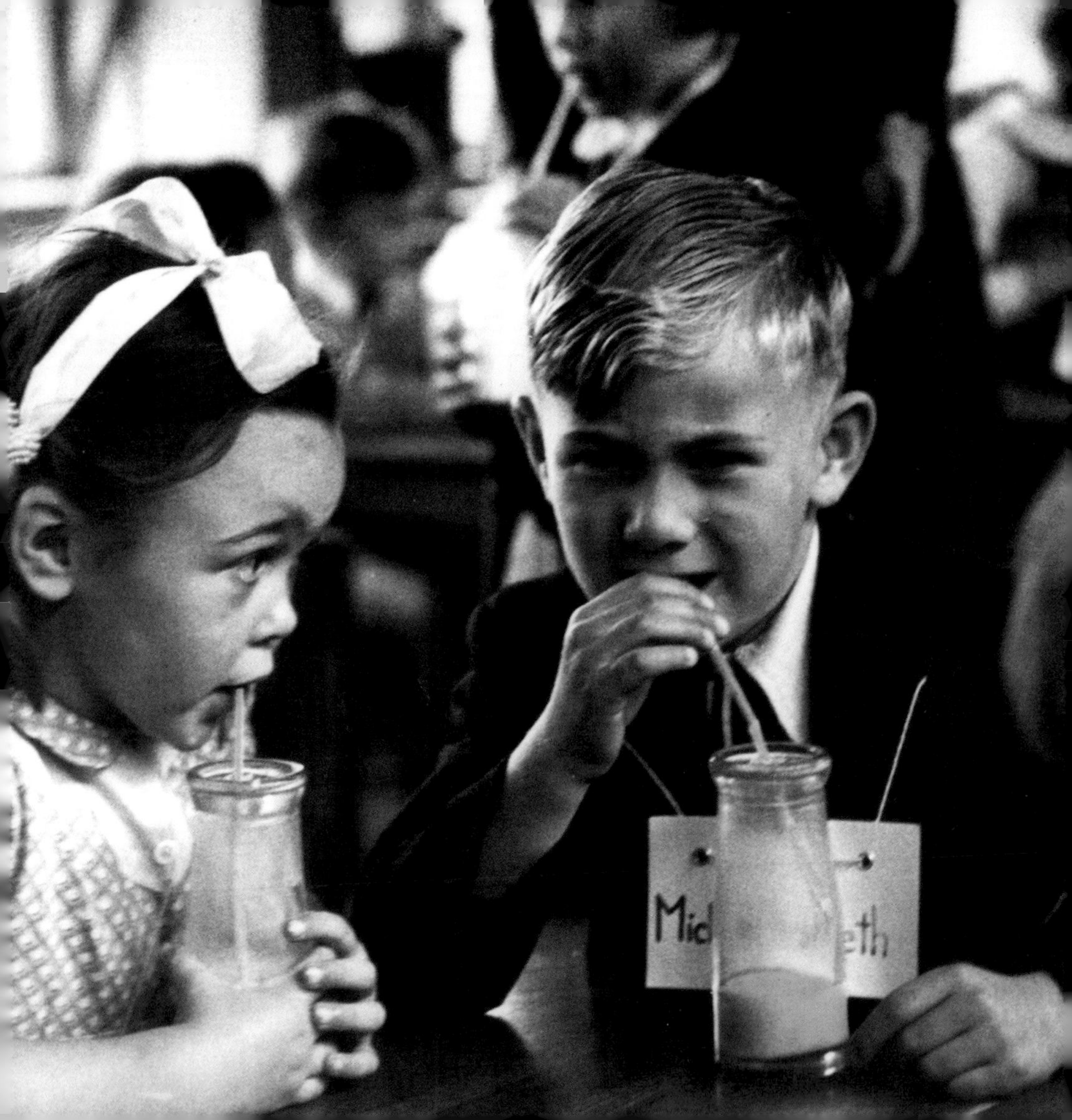
Mic
eth

LIFE IS SHORT.

When in doubt, DRINK CHOCOLATE.

Every baby should get this kind of **attention.**

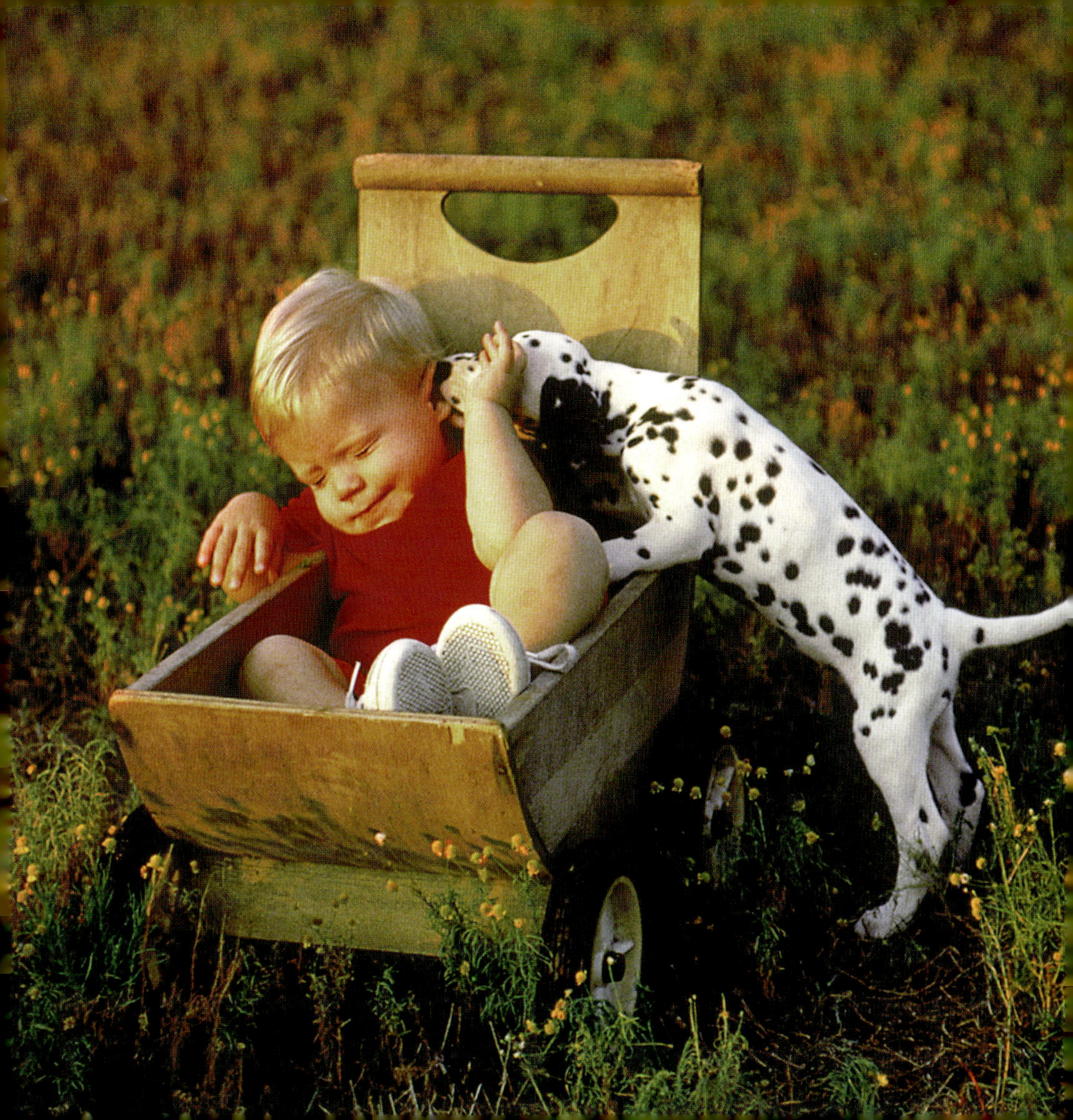

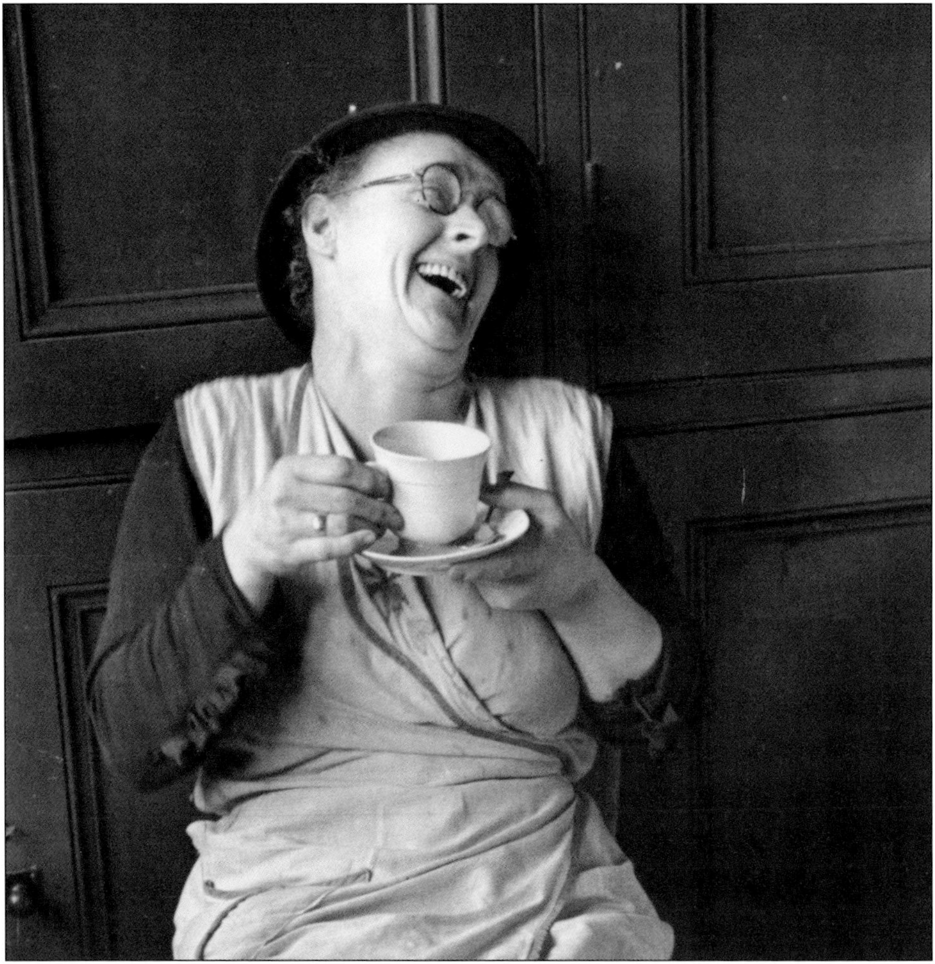

Sometimes a **COFFEE BREAK** makes everything **WORTHWHILE.**

One tiny LAUGH,

a WORLD of JOY.

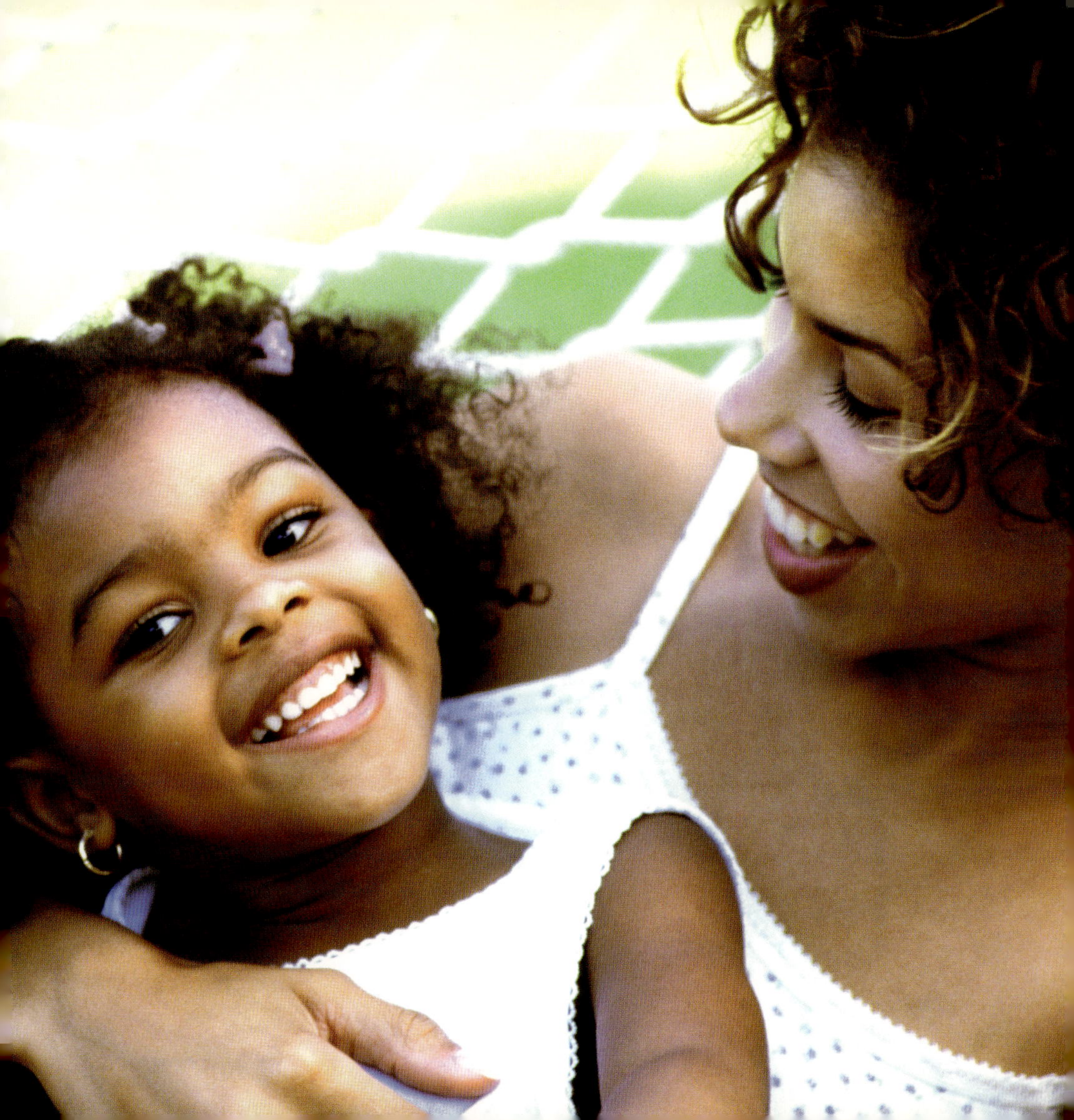

When **LIFE** gives you a TRAFFIC JAM, have a **PICNIC.**

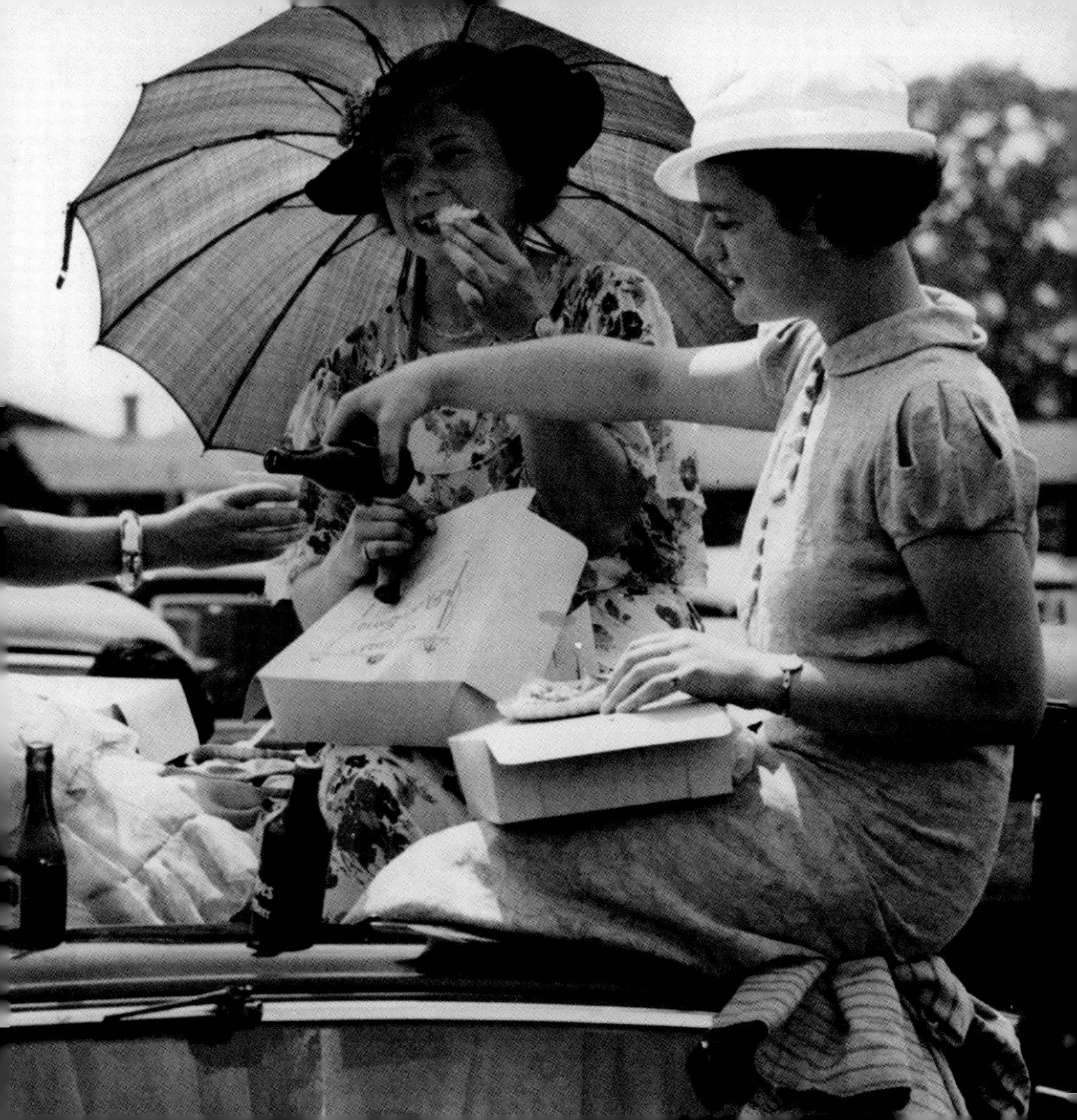

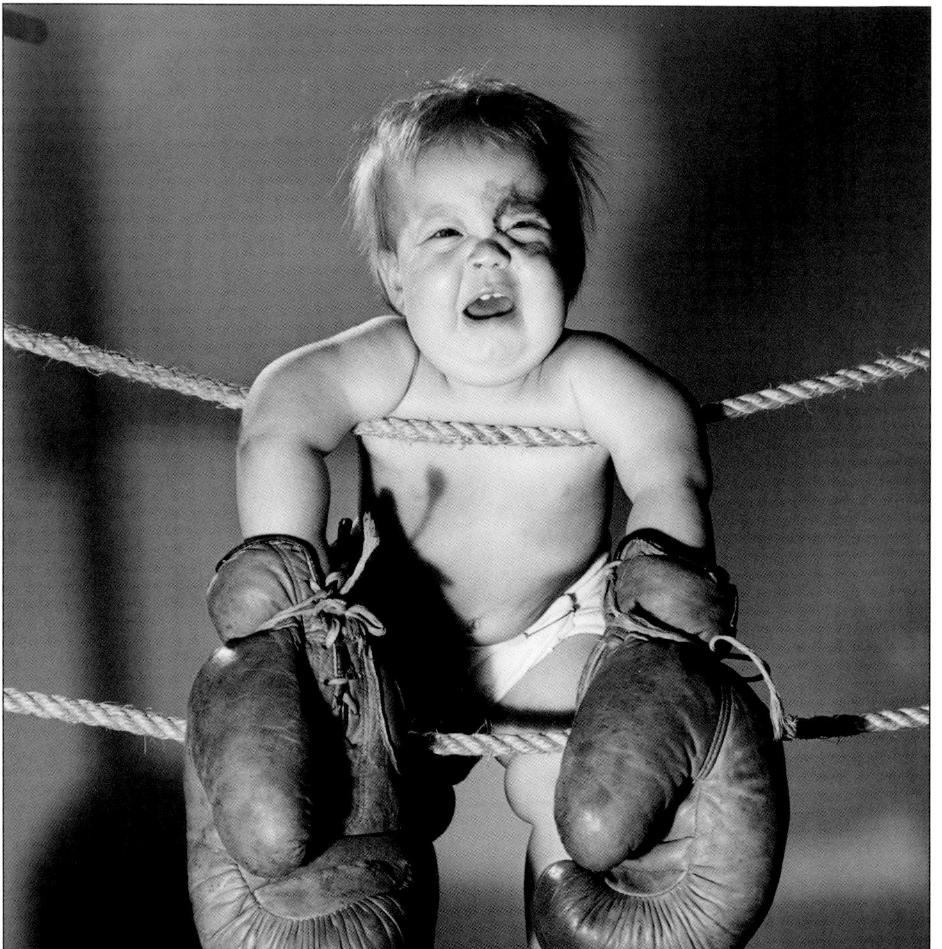

Beneath every **TOUGH-GUY** exterior, there's a LITTLE BOY crying for ATTENTION.

A quick **FLIGHT** back to **CHILDHOOD.**

Photo credits:

Front cover: **Getty Images**

Back cover: **SuperStock/Mauritius**

Age Fotostock: 14–15, 23, 29, 34, 38, 41, 48;
Getty Images: 7, 11, 12–13, 16–17, 20, 26, 30, 33, 36, 43, 50, 57, 60, 64, 68, 72–73; **Image Club:** 14; **Index Stock Imagery, Inc.:** Benelux Press, 76–77; Nathan Bilow, 52–53; Network Productions, 24–25; Lisa Rudy, 67; **PhotoDisc:** 6, 19, 22, 28, 31, 39, 49, 62, 66, 75; **SuperStock:** 44–45, 47, 74; Bruce Avery, 71; Mauritius, 8, 18, 59, 62; Kwame Zikomo, 54–55; **Brian Warling/Warling Studios:** 61.